Protecting a Sinking City

Ben Nussbaum

✸ Smithsonian

© 2019 Smithsonian Institution. The name "Smithsonian" and the Smithsonian logo are registered trademarks owned by the Smithsonian Institution.

Contributing Author

Jennifer Lawson

Consultants

Sharon Park, FAIA
Associate Director of the Smithsonian's Architectural and Historic Preservation
Smithsonian Institution

Sharon Banks
3rd Grade Teacher
Duncan Public Schools

Publishing Credits

Rachelle Cracchiolo, M.S.Ed., *Publisher*
Conni Medina, M.A.Ed., *Managing Editor*
Diana Kenney, M.A.Ed., NBCT, *Content Director*
Véronique Bos, *Creative Director*
Robin Erickson, *Art Director*
Michelle Jovin, M.A., *Associate Editor*
Mindy Duits, *Senior Graphic Designer*
Smithsonian Science Education Center

Image Credits: front cover, p.1 Horst Gerlach/iStock; p.6, p.7 NASA; p.8 (bottom) Ken Welsh/Bridgeman Images; pp.8–9 National Gallery of Art; p.11 (top) Giacomelli Photographic Archive, Venice; pp.16–17 Vincenzo Pinto/AFP/Getty Images; p.17 (top) Paul Wootton/Science Source; p.18 Sarah Hadley/Alamy; p.24 Jim West/Alamy; p.25 Air National Guard photo by Master Sgt. Toby M. Valadie; p.26 Merlin74/Shutterstock; p.27 (top) Arka Dutta/Pacific Press/LightRocket via Getty Images; p.27 (bottom) xuanhuongho/iStock; all other images from iStock/Shutterstock.

Library of Congress Cataloging-in-Publication Data

Names: Nussbaum, Ben, 1975- author.
Title: Protecting a sinking city / Ben Nussbaum.
Description: Huntington Beach, CA : Teacher Created Materials, [2019] | Includes index. | Audience: Grades K-3. |
Identifiers: LCCN 2018030484 (print) | LCCN 2018039488 (ebook) | ISBN 9781493869145 | ISBN 9781493866748
Subjects: LCSH: Venice (Italy)--Threat of destruction--Juvenile literature. | Floods--Italy--Venice--Juvenile literature. | Environmental protection--Italy--Venice--Juvenile literature.
Classification: LCC DG672.5 (ebook) | LCC DG672.5 .N87 2019 (print) | DDC 363.34/9360945311--dc23
LC record available at https://lccn.loc.gov/2018030484

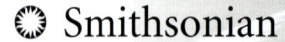

Smithsonian

© 2019 Smithsonian Institution. The name "Smithsonian" and the Smithsonian logo are registered trademarks owned by the Smithsonian Institution.

Teacher Created Materials

5301 Oceanus Drive
Huntington Beach, CA 92649-1030
www.tcmpub.com
ISBN 978-1-4938-6674-8
© 2019 Teacher Created Materials, Inc.

Table of Contents

A City of Water 4

Escape to the Lagoon 6

Building Venice 10

Saving the City 16

An American Venice 22

Water World 26

STEAM Challenge 28

Glossary 30

Index 31

Career Advice 32

A City of Water

Imagine a city of islands. Friends wave across the water to each other. There are no cars and no streets. People walk or take boats. Houses do not have green yards. Instead, front doors open to a **canal**.

This is Venice (VEN-is), Italy. It may sound like a fake city, but it is real. Once, Venice was one of the most powerful cities in the world. Now, it is fighting to survive.

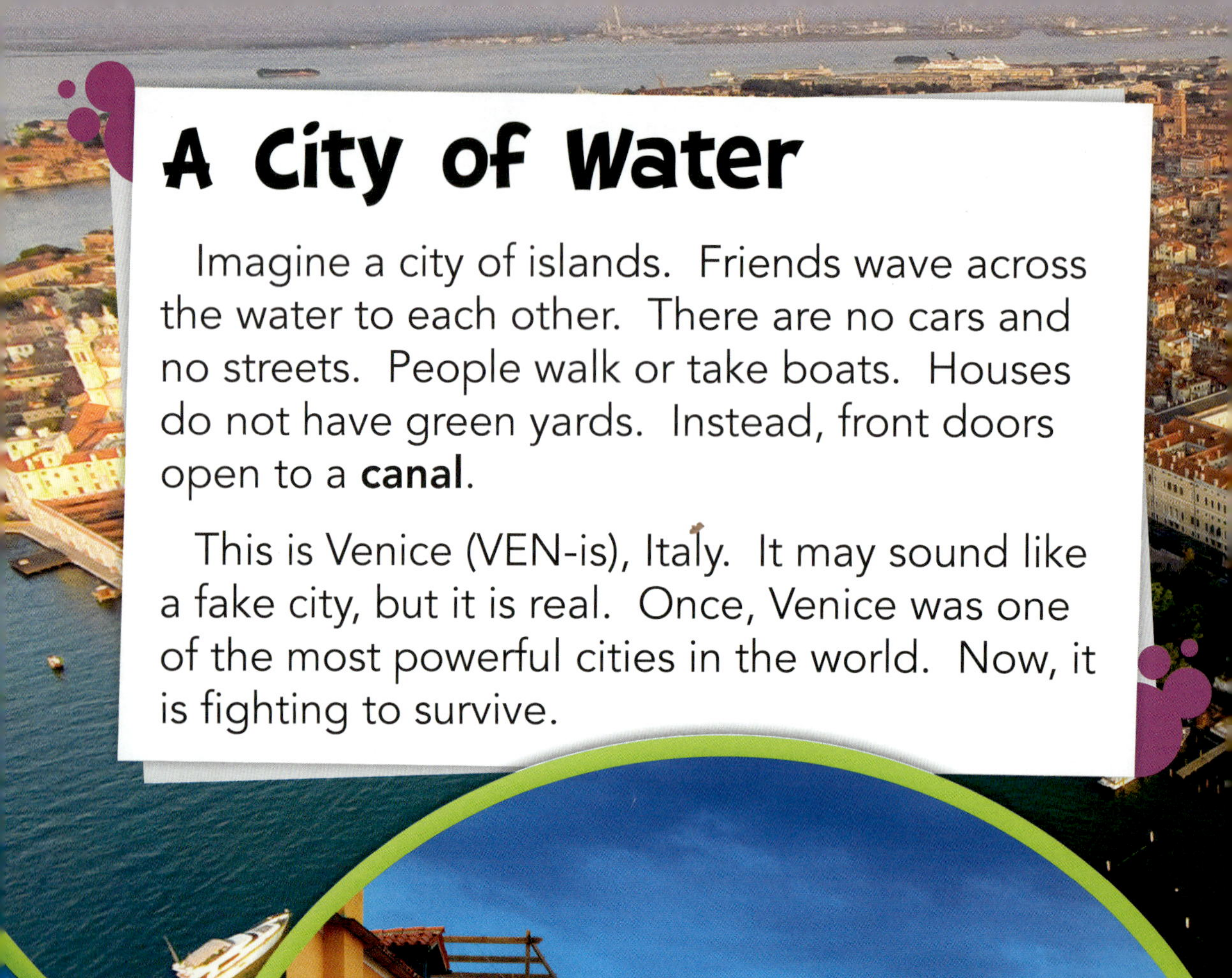

Venice, Italy, from above

The symbol of Venice is a lion with wings. It is called the Lion of St. Mark.

Escape to the Lagoon

Venice is in a **lagoon** (luh-GOON). A lagoon is an area of shallow water separated from a larger body of water. In Venice, a thin area of land makes a natural wall. This land forms the lagoon and keeps the sea from sweeping in.

For a long time, few people lived in Venice. They had a hard life. The water in the lagoon is salty, so safe drinking water was hard to find. In the summer, bugs filled the air.

Then, armies invaded an area near Venice. People fled that area. Some came to the lagoon. It became a safe place.

This photo of Venice was taken from space.

Adriatic Sea

The islands in the lagoon were wet and swampy. Building with heavy stones would be a bad idea. The weight of the stones would cause the buildings to sink into the wet ground.

Over the years, people learned how to live in Venice. Many people became traders. They bought and sold things. Ships sailed to and from the city. The **cargo** on the ships made people in Venice rich.

The city grew quickly. But it was still a city built on water. People in Venice have always had to fight the sea.

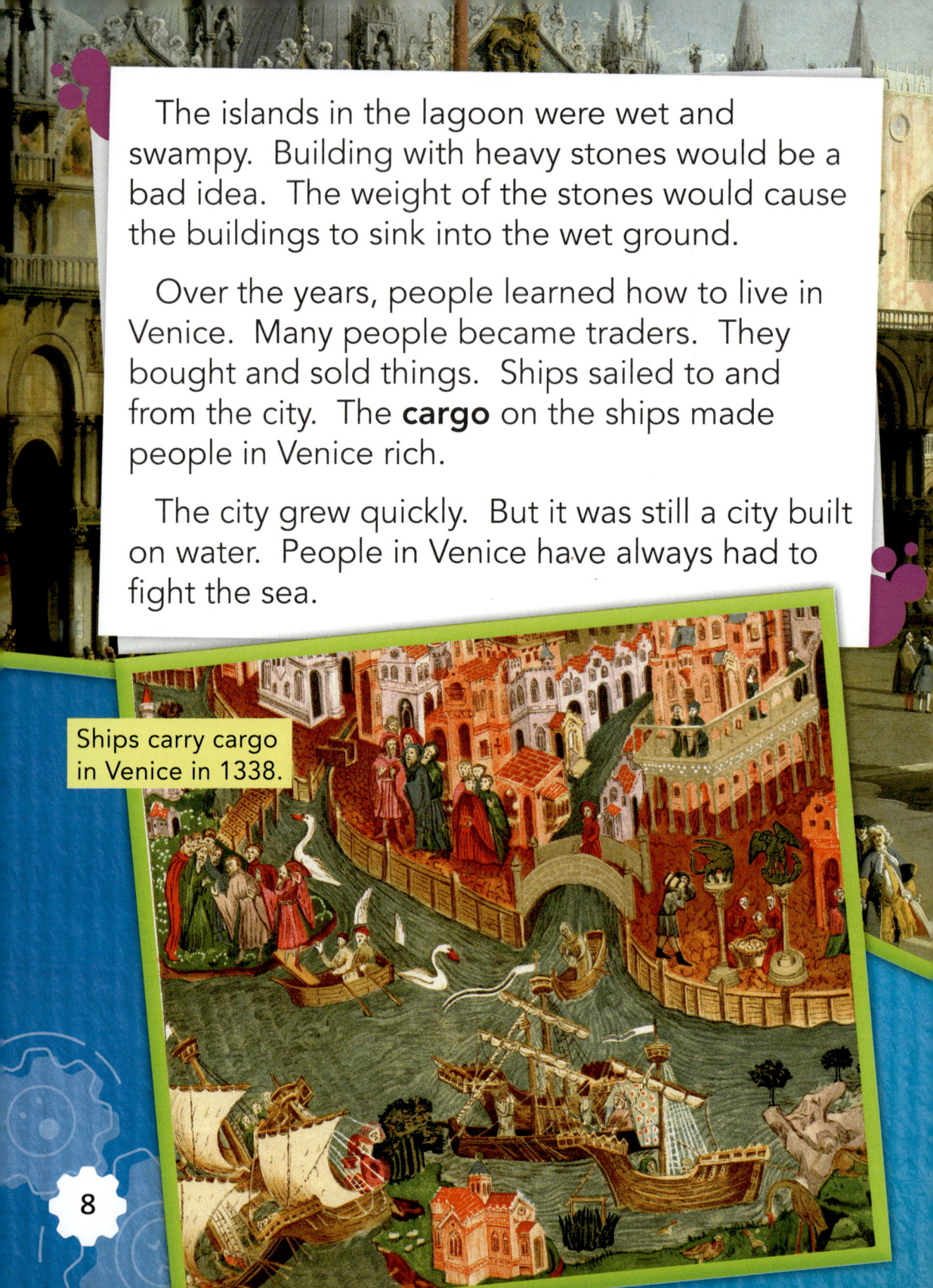

Ships carry cargo in Venice in 1338.

This painting from the 1740s shows traders in Saint Mark's Square in Venice.

Venice used to be its own country. People have lived in the area since around AD 568.

Building Venice

All over the world, people build near water or even right on top of it. Stilt houses are one way to do so. People bury wooden poles deep in the wet earth and then build on top of them.

Venice is a city full of stilt houses. The stilts cannot be seen, but they hold up the city. Some of the poles Venice sits on top of are very long. They go past the water, past the mud, and deep into the hard clay. These long poles help keep the buildings steady.

stilt houses in Chile

This 1780 painting shows builders from Venice burying poles into the clay.

Science

Oh No, Oxygen

Wood can rot when it comes into contact with **oxygen** (AHK-sih-juhn), which is in air and water. But over the years, silt and soil have forced their way into Venice's poles. This has made the poles as hard as stone. The poles were also placed close together in the clay. These things keep them from rotting.

There are many poles under Venice, holding up the city. On top of the poles, people put a layer of wood. On top of the wood, they put a few layers of stone. Then, they built houses. In Venice, bricks are thin or hollow. This helps keep the houses light.

People use **mortar** to hold bricks in place. In Venice, the mortar is a little flexible. This is a key detail. Wet soil changes its shape over time. Houses in Venice have to move a little as the poles shift in the wet soil. The flexible mortar lets buildings move without falling over.

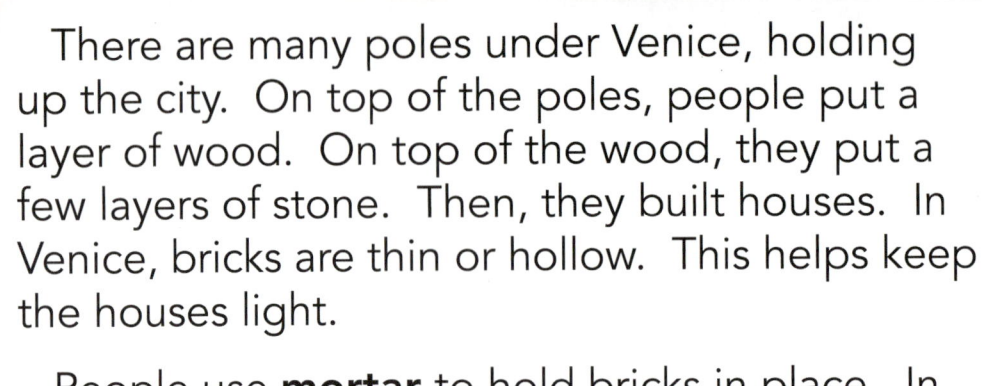

Stilt House in Venice
- water level
- layer of stone
- layer of wood
- mud
- poles in firm clay

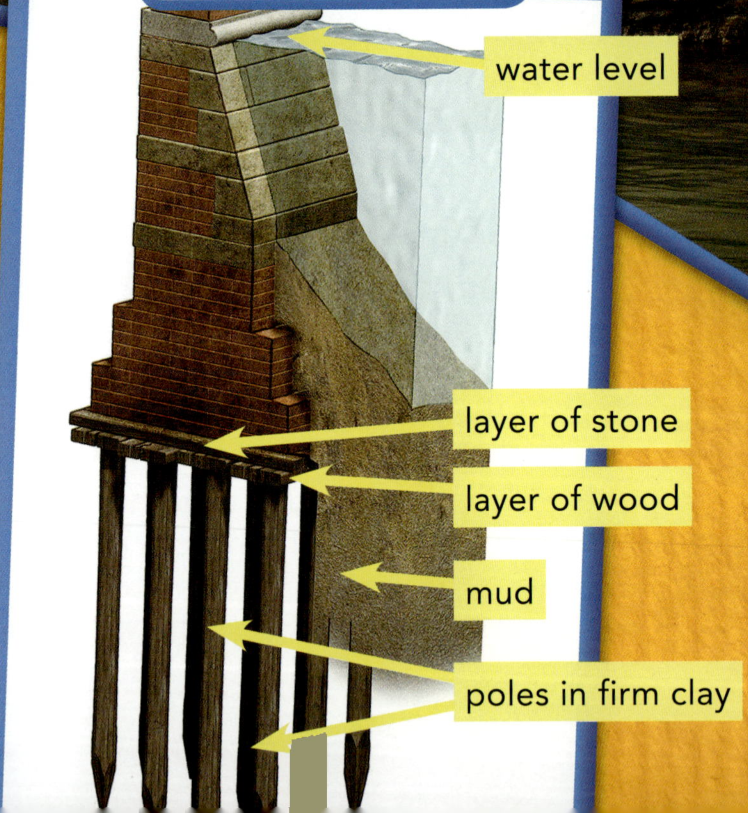

mortar

Today, Venice is full of old buildings. Some have sat on top of the water for more than five hundred years. People come from all over to admire this city of water.

But some buildings are not safe. Venice has been sinking for many years. The wet, soft ground under Venice is shifting. The sea is rising too. This can cause flooding. In many homes, the ground floor is empty to keep people safe from flooding.

Venice is in trouble. People are working to protect it before it is too late.

Saint Mark's Square flooded in 2015.

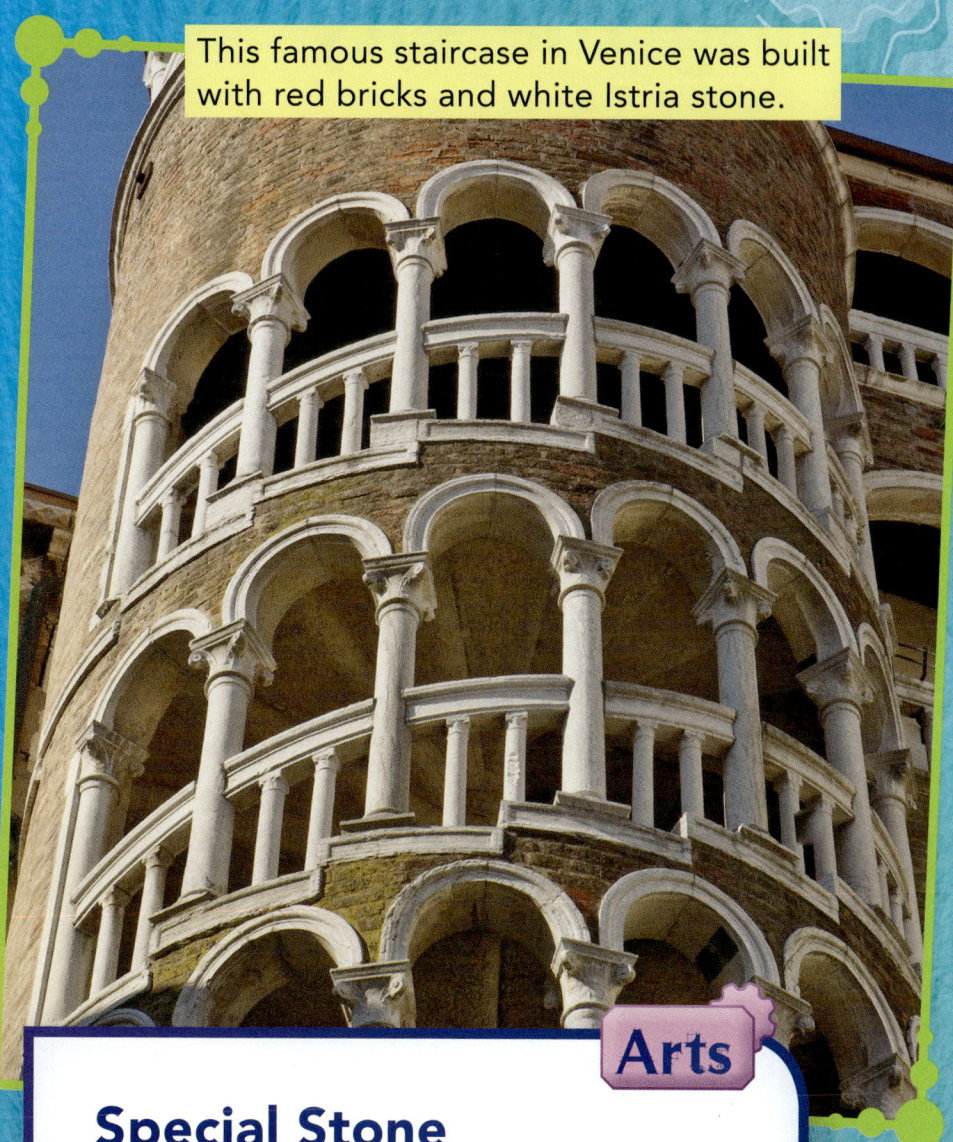

This famous staircase in Venice was built with red bricks and white Istria stone.

Arts

Special Stone

Istria (IS-tree-uh) stone is used in many places in Venice. The white stone stays strong in water. It also adds to the city's beauty. The stone looks like expensive marble. Istria stone also stands out from red bricks.

Saving the City

Venice will not be saved by any one person. People have to work together. For one project, Italy's government teamed up with builders and **engineers**. They looked to the city's **inlets**. The inlets let boats and fish in and out of the lagoon. But the inlets are also causing problems.

The inlet system uses six walls to stop major flooding. But some walls are **rusting** from the sea air. Other walls will not rise when they are supposed to. People are working to fix these things. But it is costing a lot of money. Some people want to give up on the walls.

This wall rises out of the water to stop flooding.

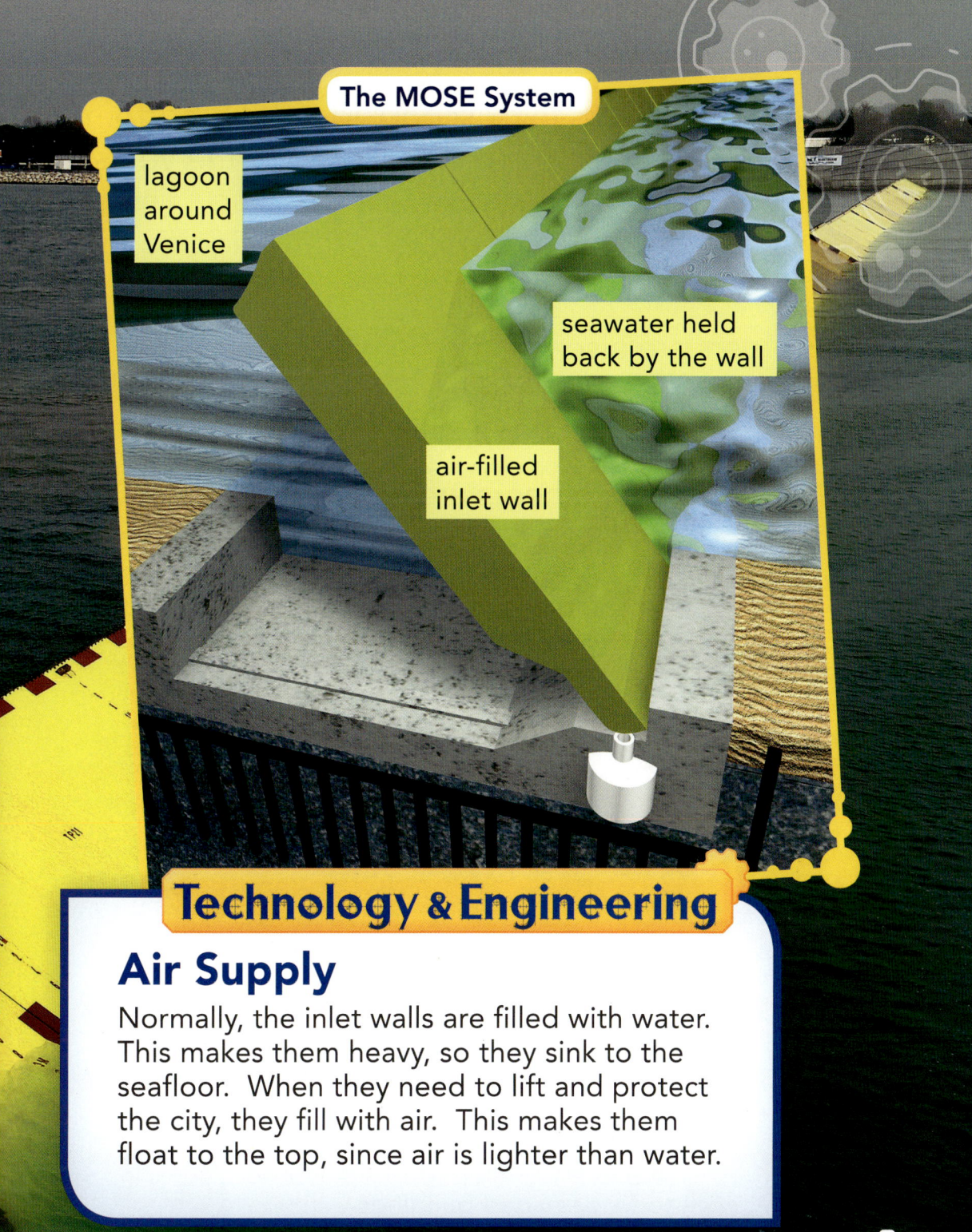

The MOSE System

- lagoon around Venice
- seawater held back by the wall
- air-filled inlet wall

Technology & Engineering

Air Supply

Normally, the inlet walls are filled with water. This makes them heavy, so they sink to the seafloor. When they need to lift and protect the city, they fill with air. This makes them float to the top, since air is lighter than water.

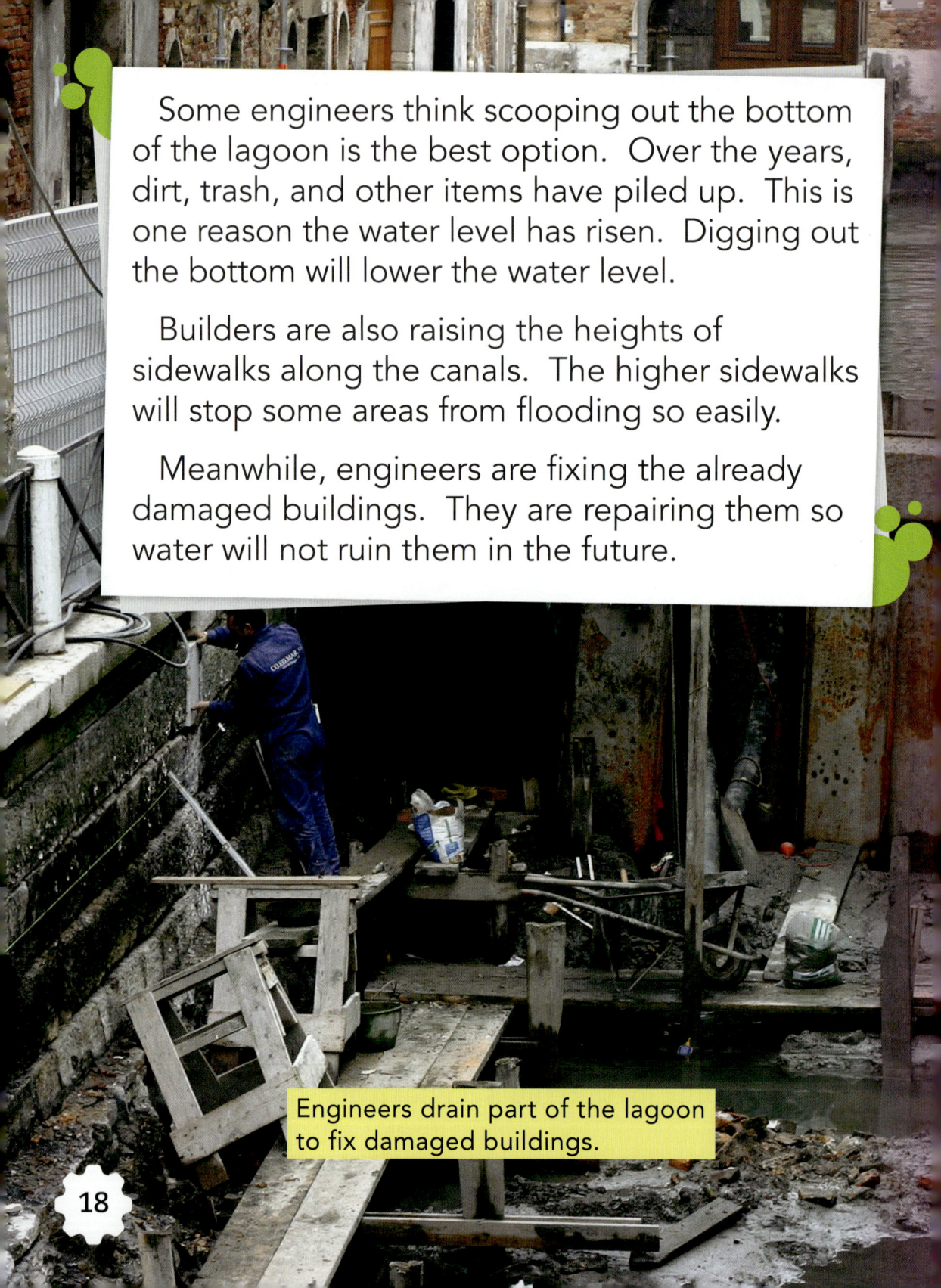

Some engineers think scooping out the bottom of the lagoon is the best option. Over the years, dirt, trash, and other items have piled up. This is one reason the water level has risen. Digging out the bottom will lower the water level.

Builders are also raising the heights of sidewalks along the canals. The higher sidewalks will stop some areas from flooding so easily.

Meanwhile, engineers are fixing the already damaged buildings. They are repairing them so water will not ruin them in the future.

Engineers drain part of the lagoon to fix damaged buildings.

As builders dig down, they have to rebuild many of the walls.

Mathematics

Lowering and Raising

Engineers and builders plan to save buildings by lowering the water level of the lagoon and raising the sidewalks. The plan is to dig down about 180 centimeters (6 feet) into the lagoon floor. Then, builders would raise the sidewalks about 120 cm (4 ft.). These plans would add about 300 cm (10 ft.) of distance between the water and the sidewalks.

Engineers also learned that people used to take water from Venice's **aquifers**. The water was used to power machines. It helped Venice grow.

But taking out water left gaps. Before, the water acted as a cushion between bits of **sediment**. After, the bits of sediment could pack closer together. As a result, the ground sank.

Engineers now want to add water back into the sand beneath the city. They hope the ground will swell up. They think it will lift the city.

Venice is being used as a test. What works there might work in other places.

Engineers in California used water to swell the soil and lift a city in the 1960s.

Aquifer Layers in Venice

An American Venice

Like Venice, other cities around the world fight water. One of those cities is New Orleans. It is famous for its music and food.

Water surrounds this U.S. city. Rivers, lakes, and the sea are all nearby. There are swamps and marshes too. These areas are known as wetlands. They are filled with wildlife. They are special places.

The wetlands protect the city. Strong storms come in from the sea. The storms pass over the wetlands first. They lose some strength before they hit the city. But New Orleans is facing a problem—its wetlands are disappearing.

Jackson Square in New Orleans faces the Mississippi River.

New Orleans, Louisiana, is surrounded by rivers and lakes.

This roseate spoonbill depends on the wetlands.

People have ruined New Orleans' wetlands. Some people wrecked wetlands to make it easier for ships to pass through. Other people wanted to make it easier to live in the city.

People did not know how much damage they were doing. Now, they are trying to save the wetlands. Engineers are working hard to rebuild these areas. They are returning them to the way they used to be. This process is very hard. It also costs a lot of money. But saving them is important.

A volunteer replants cypress trees in the wetlands.

A helicopter creates a natural wall with trees in New Orleans.

A group of volunteers rebuilds the New Orleans' coastline.

Water World

Many people live near water. If the sea keeps rising, they will be in trouble. Their homes could be destroyed. Their stores and schools could flood. It will take a lot of people working together to save them.

People are working very hard to help cities like Venice. They know that if Venice can survive, so can other places. That is why it is important to protect this sinking city.

This statue in Venice urges people to save the lagoon from rising sea levels.

People in Vietnam ride motorbikes through flooded streets.

A woman in India stands near her sinking home.

STEAM CHALLENGE

Define the Problem

Many stilt houses in Venice are in trouble. You have been asked to design and build a model for a new type of house. Your house should sit above the water. It should keep people safe from flooding.

 **Constraints:** Your house must be at least 25 centimeters (10 inches) tall.

 **Criteria:** Your house must stay upright on its own. Your house must stay dry when placed in 8 cm (3 in.) of water.

1. Research and Brainstorm

How do houses in Venice stand in water? How are engineers trying to save Venice? What makes houses in Venice so sturdy?

2. Design and Build

Sketch your design of your house. What purpose will each part serve? What materials will work best? Build the model.

3. Test and Improve

Measure your house. Is it at least 25 cm (10 in.) tall? Place your model in 8 cm (3 in.) of water. Is your house above the water? Is it sturdy? How can you improve it? Improve your design and try again.

4. Reflect and Share

What other materials could you use? How would your design change if the water was moving? How could you add technology to your house to warn homeowners of flooding?

Glossary

aquifers—layers of sand or rock that can take in and hold water

canal—a long, narrow place that is filled with water

cargo—something that is carried from one place to another

engineers—people who use science to design solutions for problems or needs

inlets—narrow areas of water that go into land

lagoon—an area of shallow water that is separated from a larger body of water

mortar—a substance that is spread between bricks or stones to hold them together

oxygen—part of the air, which has no color, taste, or smell

rusting—forming a reddish substance on metal from coming into contact with moisture or air

sediment—very small pieces of rock, such as sand, gravel, and dust

Index

cargo, 8
Chile, 10
India, 27
inlets, 16–17
Istria stone, 15
Italy, 4–5, 7, 16
Lion of St. Mark, 5
mortar, 12–13
New Orleans, 22–25
oxygen, 11

Saint Mark's Square, 9, 14
stilt houses, 10, 12
Vietnam, 27
wetlands, 22–24

Career Advice
from Smithsonian

Do you want to protect sinking cities? Here are some tips to get you started.

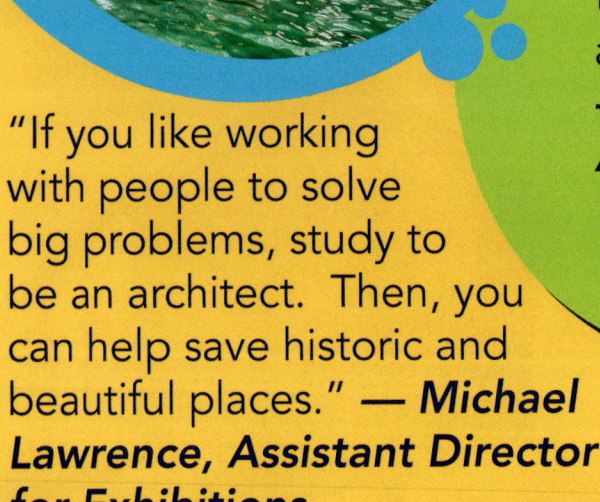

"Study architecture. Learn how buildings are built to withstand water. Then, you take care of cities and buildings."
—*Sharon Park, Associate Director*

"If you like working with people to solve big problems, study to be an architect. Then, you can help save historic and beautiful places." — *Michael Lawrence, Assistant Director for Exhibitions*